THE E

Written

Photographs by John Paul Endress

WANTED: A gardener to care for my _____ plant

orn

arn

ern

OK

Celebration Press

Parsippany, New Jersey

Can you see the words on the board? No!

Let's go to the eye doctor.

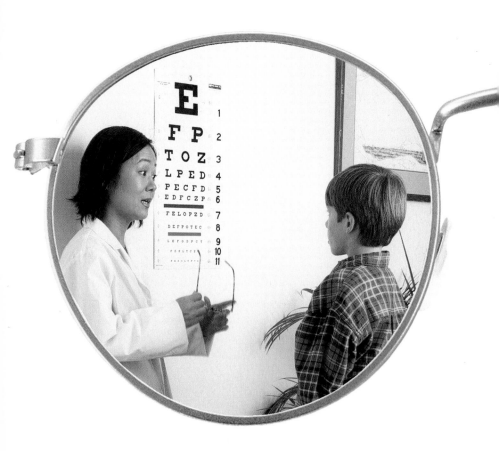

The eye doctor uses an eye chart.

The eye doctor uses eye drops.

The eye doctor checks your eyes.

The eye doctor says, "You need glasses!"

Can you see the words on the board? Yes!